BROKEN PIECES

GABRIEL EMMANUEL DESINCE

MISSION
POSSIBLE
PRESS

MISSION POSSIBLE PRESS
Creating Legacies through Absolute Good Works

The Mission is Possible.
Sharing love and wisdom for the young and "the young at heart,"
expanding minds, restoring kindness through good thoughts,
feelings, and attitudes is our intent. May you thrive and be good
in all you are and all you do...
Be Cause U.R. Absolute Good!

Broken Pieces
© 2019 Gabriel Emmanuel Desince

Books may be purchased in quantity by contacting the publisher
directly:
Mission Possible Press, A division of Absolute Good
PO Box 8039 St. Louis, MO 63156
or by calling 240.644.2500
MissionPossiblePress.com

ISBN   978-0-9996766-8-4
First Edition

DEDICATION

This book is dedicated to my mom, Kim Fonseca and my little sister Trinity Joy Fonseca.

ACKNOWLEDGEMENT

To everyone who feels like they have to say, something that's hard to get out, something that they just don't know how to express so they hold it in. This is for you...

CONTENTS

BROKEN PIECES

I've come to terms with my brokenness,
like the careless hands that drop glass to its shattering
demise.

These are the same hands that quickly conjure a broom to
ward the shards away.

You see my brokenness is that one remaining piece of glass
that goes unnoticed.

The one that hides from light and vision all the same, only
to abruptly remind me, it is there, when I least expect it,
when I've let my guard down and my feet are bare.

My brokenness has drawn blood on many occasions.

A POEM CALLED ME

I was born May 9th, 1990 some say that makes me a Taurus.
I don't care for horoscopes but most
believe my sign makes me hard headed.

My entire dichotomy is gift wrapped in irony.
I'm shorter than most,
yet I always stick out
like bright colors amongst dull backdrops.

I prefer that metaphor
because the phrase "sticks out like a sore thumb" reminds
me of pain.

I hate pain.

Yet I know hurt all too well.

My weaknesses are bubbly women and sweets.

There is irony to that.

I have two missing fathers that I haven't forgiven
and one Father who forgave me for killing His Son.

At night I go on long rides accompanied by empty car seats
and music that fights with the silent air for the space that my
vessel isn't filling.

I'm filled with grief, joy, patience, love, kindness, passion, anger, despair, and hope, but the greatest of these is love.
So, therefore, I carry God in me.
So But some days He's so quiet I forget He's there.

I often find myself whispering,
"Pssssst! *Hey are You in there? Because I really need you out here in these streets.*"

I think God waits for me to go to sleep
because that's when I'm the least distracted.

That's when I'm still.
And the ins and outs of the air in my chest sounds like the brass section of an orchestra in His ears.

It's then that my dreams are filled with Him telling me my reality can be as well.

SLAVES AND VICES

I see bent and broken shadows
of former Kings and Queens
chained to occupying the station
of the basement.

Like the chocolate figurines of our history bent over in lowly
positions hovering atop yay high cotton trees.

With each feeble pluck of produce
those white puffs picked by agonizing worker bees pollinating
the fruit of the loom,
a ball of cotton turns into a 5th of vodka, henn, pills, and
moonshine distilled.

During nights of washing away the gloom
leave Kings draped over park benches like throws over
couches in living rooms.

Slaves still waiting to be emancipated.

ON THE EVENING NEWS

A homeless man was found hanging from a tree today.
Since we are all made in God's image,
reflections of God's resemblance,
you could say God was found hanging from a tree today.

I heard the news and found myself dismayed,
in the thick of the fray,
my thoughts began forming cumulus and nimbus clouds
above my sulking shroud forecasting a 100 percent chance
of rain.

A few raindrops found their way down my cheeks taking
leaps of faith off the edge of my face,
only to make watermarks on thrifted apparel.
And like the glimmer of light beams through dark clouds on
grim days,
so was an old familiar tune that pierced the sorrowful fray.

WHAT HAPPENS TO A DREAM?

I was 17 then. Back when I got a girl's number, called her up and awkwardly muddled through subjects until eventually, we both were okay with either making a joke about everything or hearing each other's breath whisper into the phone line. In these moments time was irrelevant, until we got off the phone, looked at the alarm clock and realized we only had 3 hours left before we had to get on the morning school bus.

At 17 I thought I had it all figured out.

When don't we think we have it all figured out? But the thing about youth is that we pondered over who we were going to be.

I remember being on the phone with a crush. Whether she knew I was crushing or didn't know, I can't really remember. What I do remember is how free and open my heart was to some of the grandest of possibilities. I mean like that Aladdin, "I can show you the world," kind of feeling.

The conversation sort of went like, "What do you wanna do when you grow up?" I asked.

She said, "I don't really know, what do you wanna do?"

I guess I had been squirming, waiting for someone to ask me such a simple question. It was that final twist to a shaken up bottle of soda. With the release of the built up pressure of all my dreams and schemes. I told her, "I wanna help people, but not like a doctor or counselor. I wanna touch millions of people! I always have these visions and glimpses of seeing myself on a stage in front of millions of people, but I never really see exactly what I'm doing, I just know it's big!"

She reacted as if soda had burst over her.

When soda bursts, most people are shocked at the bursting as they wipe their clothing, and then proceed to enjoy what remains of the beverage.

She was silent for a second which was the shock. She then said, "Wow."

The wiping of the clothing. "That's a big dream."

Drinking what's left, "I believe you can do that."

Satisfaction outweighed the shock. I grew up dreaming big and wondering why people around didn't often do the same. The thing about life is that sometimes dreams get deferred.

Langston Hughes wondered what happened to such dreams in "Harlem":

What happens to a dream deferred?

Does it dry up like a raisin in the sun?
Or fester like a sore—And then run?
Does it stink like rotten meat?
Or crust and sugar over—like a syrupy sweet?

Maybe it just sags
like a heavy load.
Or does it explode?

10 years later I soul search in an effort to answer the same questions.

SPECTRE: GHOST OF GIRLFRIENDS PAST

Sometimes you haunt me like a Ghost of Girlfriends Past,
a fragment of what didn't last between us.

In between us lies land, wind, and sea.
The air we breathe.
Time, mass, and frequencies.
Yet frequently you frequent me to steal my peace.

I'd hoped you would've faded peacefully,
but sometimes you haunt me.
Like a familiar fragrance
whose source is unseen.
A lingering vagrant
loitering the premises.
An entity entering my dreams
to my unaware expectancy.

Now my expectations expect you to come and leave
because sometimes you haunt me.
Sometimes you taunt me.
The recesses of my heart want relief from the relentless
reappearances of your appearance.

I deemed our former experiences unredeemable,
inconceivable even to my imagination, yet a
reanimation of you remains animated in me.

Somehow because sometimes you haunt me.

CATERPILLAR STANCE

Am I protecting my creative assets?
Am I ready to reveal my greatest achievement?
Am I to withdraw to heal?
To grow?
Am I to create something new?
Am I to search my soul before moving forward?
Does my real identity contain the truth?
Am I worthy to grab hold to my calling?
Am I to practice more sensitivity to what matters in my
vicinity?
Am I to see the positivity that is potentially all around me?

You see...
you see,
I am to be transformed by the renewing of my mind.
So on the outside one may gaze
upon a caterpillar in short-sightedness,
but on the inside, I bare the nature
of the butterfly in all of its likeness.

Acquainted with pain!
Destined for challenge!
Subject to change!
Created for growth!
What beauty to gain!

With a propensity toward grace I bare the nature
of the butterfly
with patient expectancy and hope,
faithfully this promise spurs me
To cope...
Cope...
Cope with my present condition this body of death!

Who will save me from its affliction?!
As I fight fictional apparitions
of never being
commissioned to the mission
of finding success in achieving
my God-given inner disposition.
To fly.
To become the butterfly.

To be continued...

BY WAY OF COCOON

Subdued in seclusion,
safeguarded from intrusion.

This silence is violent!
This silence is violent!
This silence is violent!

It magnifies my every thought.
Merciless seems the intent
in which the butterfly is wrought.
Must the old me be sold
for the new me to be bought?

The enveloping darkness
yields no response.

A slave I'll succumb
to the new nature, I'll become.

Growing pains,
growing pains,
growing pains,
inflicted by the changing of my frame.

WRITER'S BLOCK

I spent many hours rebuking
the devil in the details.
Do tell the tale with all honesty.
I have failed to manufacture
a manuscript meant for mentioning
more or less the mesmerizing
of mortified minds
mystified by the mystery
of the Maker.
To make matters worse, I remain trapped in mine.

Mind my manners but my mannerisms have maintained a
movement that remains minute.

Consistency molasses
In other words
stagnant.
Unable to produce a writ
hindered by the rigor mortis
that has ravaged my wrist.

In my world
the pen and the paper
refuse to coexist
cursed,
Writer's Block!

A HARLOT SPEAKS OF HOLINESS

I know men.
I know magis, magistrates, ministers, and monks alike.
I know men of piety, in need of sobriety, rejects of society.
I know men.
I know men in high places, I know men in low places.

The faces all seem a blur when the memories occur.
A face doesn't make a man different.
I'd defer to the good book that says none are righteous
they all need the Spirit.

None are righteous except one.
None are righteous except the Son.
He died for me,
on that tree He cried for me,
and I find that He's the only man that'll ever love me.
But truthfully,
I'm out here doing me.

And besides Jesus I need the love of
Benjamin Franklin, Thomas Jefferson, George Washington,
Alexander Hamilton, Abraham Lincoln, and Andrew Jackson.

Jackson keeps me fed,
Lincoln feeds the preacher man,
Hamilton appeases Uncle Sam,
and Franklin keeps a roof over my head.

Once all that holy stuff is said,
the way I see it, I'm stained
either with the blood of Jesus or my disobedience.
I was born with rot, I lack the ingredients to believe in such
a credence.

See, it's gonna take holiness like the sea to diminish the
blemishes on me.
But for now
this make up will have to do.

THE PROMISED LAND

I speak of the promised land
I speak of beauty in its
features.

Featurettes of sunsets and beaches
where the grass is always greener.
Full of peaches and cream
the burial ground of deferred dreams and defeated dreamers.
The schemers say it's the place they want to be.

In their own skin being wannabes.
I speak of the promised land.
Wherein lies the palisades of those who complain
where plains of ripe fruit hang in plain sight.
Here strange sight denies natives their
birthrights.

Plights of agony air alongside
sounds of laughing babies
maybe they can't see the struggle as mommy and daddy does.

I speak of the promised land
And those willing to ride or die for it.
An eye for an eye for it.
To forge their destinies,
desperately seeking its riches.
Success in their ventures is all they ever breathe.

No other notion could ever be conceived
outside of conquest.

They will never rest until the land is arrested and its promises
are manifested as monetary investments.
I speak of the promised land.

THE WEIGHT OF THE WORLD

Today the weight of the world fell on my shoulders
and I crumbled under it.
Folded my hands
threw out my back
buckled my knees
and tasted defeat.

Defeat gritted between my teeth and
my face was on terrible two year old.
Momma is making me eat all my veggies again.
That day the weight of the world fell on my shoulders
I hated those veggies.

But I'm much older now and my problems are boulders now
and the world is colder now.
It's enough to catch pneumonia or a fade whichever comes first.
Hopefully not in that order,
Camcorder, camcorder record me in this land of disorder.

Someone save me and come back for Private Ryan.
I can't believe I'm so selfish.

One day the weight of the world fell on my shoulders
and I pretended like I was the only one.

Like struggle isn't a team effort
like we all aren't rocking the jerseys with humanity on the
front.

MUSTARD SEED

In *Imax* 3D you placed a glimpse of your dream in front of me.
Your vision light projected throughout the room like movie nights.

You painted such a picture with broad brush strokes.
A Van Gogh with your words,
And I sat childlike.
It doesn't take much to mystify toddler faith.

You told me it doesn't take much to tell mountains
to excuse me, you're in my way, go kick rocks!

You never measured your lifetime in ticks and tocks,
but in risk and stocks and things unseen to the natural eye.
A supernatural life
because to you it never took much to invest love.

Graceful as a dove and wise.
I've never known a person
whose leaps of faith looked more like synchronized dives.

With an ability to share your will to succeed,
yet so casual.
So one day you casually popped open a bag of mustard seeds.
One fell on fertile soil and
that soil was me.

I'll always remember the dream.

TIMES I'VE BEEN IN LOVE

I can count on both hands
the number of times I fell in love.

Well maybe more like the number of times
I took nosedives off the edge of the planet into
nothingness.

It's funny,
the things I think about when I have too much
time on my hands.

Or I'm using these fingers to do basic addition and
subtraction
as I count the mistakes I made.

I guess I prefer doing the math on my fingers instead of in
my head, maybe it's because I rather not think about the
number of times I've been in love.

Because this math takes two hands, ten fingers,
and five knuckles covered in paint, drywall, and blood.

59 TEARS

No one wakes up saying today is the day I'm going to die.
God have mercy on the souls
of the Las Vegas 59.

I write this with 59 tears in my eyes
for the 59 lives now standing outside of heaven's gates
in a single-file line.

I can't help but wonder how God feels on His throne as He
watches mankind.

Did He weep over Columbine?
Or the hate crime of Charleston that took 9?

Could Stephen Craig Paddock
Eric Harris
Dylann Roof
And Dylan Klebold
Be bold enough to look God in His eyes?
The way they gazed at their victims from behind shotguns,
semis, and loaded 9's.

No one wakes up saying
today is the day I'm going to die.

But we are quick to blame God if our loved ones
don't make it home alive
or protest if police claim another black life
or if the government continues to allow guns to power crime.

Level with me.

When tragedy happens
we are quick to form a conspiracy
point the finger, play the blame game, but we rarely
practice empathy.

Or hold people accountable to self-responsibility.

Maybe that day someone's judgment was clouded by being
ill mentally.

And God it was Your fault for letting him or her get taken
from me.

No one wakes up saying today is the day I'm going to die.
So why can't we wake up and say today I'll live fully alive?
Look our neighbor in the eye and say I value your life.

THE SEARCH

My eyes are magnifying glasses
on a mission to magnify
existence outside of my own.

An eternal being
with eternity stitched into
my chromosomes.

If eyes are the windows into the soul,
then apparently such transparency allows you
to peer and behold,
a hole designed for the whole universe to fit up in it.

Then take that universe and quantify it by an infinite number
of digits, divide it from time and multiples of mass and space.

Then question how the divine can room and board in the
most finite of places.
The search has now narrowed to what has been staring
directly in our faces.

The image of God,
not a mirrored mirage,
or makeshift mural manufactured by man,
but the One Eternal.

Constantly communicating
I AM.
I AM the one you truly seek,
I AM the alpha and the omega,
I AM the truth you see,
I AM the puzzle piece,
I AM what fits in the whole inside your chest cavity,
I AM the start and the finisher,
The furnisher of finite fractions of me.

Faithfully waiting for the day you finally see,
not with just your eyes of course,
but with the heart first and foremost,
So make the most out of the time you're given.

To dwell in your fleshly prisons
until the day I judge your eternal decision.

Either to believe in Me -
or spend eternity searching for Me in fiery furnace heat.

UNCONFESSED

I hope you get this letter.
And every word, sentence, and paragraph that you read
lets you know it's not just ink that you see, but love that I
bleed
pierced by arrows unseen
shot by heavenly beings
on a Saturday evening
when I was left stumbling
leaking at the sight of you...

I pretended to kneel down and tie my shoe
just to keep my cool
but from that point of view
all I could think of was "Will you's"
turning into "Yes's" turning into "I do's."

I stood back up on my own two
and two stepped toward you
then kept it cordial.

Totally oblivious you played your role like
"Will you be shopping with us again?"
"Yes."
"Would you like a rewards card?"
"I Do."

You won't get this letter
nor see that every word, sentence, and paragraph here to read
is not just ink to be seen,
but love that I bleed
pierced by arrows unseen
shot by heavenly beings
on a Saturday evening
when I left stumbling
mumbling over my words at the sight of you
unsure what to do
Because I had never encountered a being such as you.

So I ran to regroup
now I'm running from the truth
this letter is proof I chose the coward's way out,
cowering behind parchment, ink, scribblings, and doubt
knowing you'd respect real if it came straight from the
horse's mouth.

The verdict's out.

Ironically I considered my feeble attempts asinine.
Made not a single attempt to get your line
Then wrote this letter and made it mine.

EBONY AND IVORY

She had dark red hair stained with a tinge of brown as if she mixed coffee and cranberry juice together then dyed her hair with it. Her soft baby blue eyes seemed drawn onto a fair and speckled canvas. You could play connect the dots with her freckles and end up with quite a few distinct designs. She was a good ol' girl. Really sweet and really attractive. She always wore jeans that complimented her frame, brown cowboy boots, and a hunting camouflage jacket that allowed a Confederate flag t-shirt to peak out amidst the foliage of trees, leaves, and *Realtree* emblems.

Yes, I found her attractive and no matter how different I was, I was always able to admire beauty no matter how it came. I saw her a few times in automotive class next door to my shop class. She worked like she was one of the guys and knew when to talk out of her colon like one as well. But she always found her way back to her soft and sweet self. Every once and a while she would come by shop class and pester a few of the guys she knew with jokes and memories from backwood parties where underaged participants learned that the moon could shine in mason jars. Such activities were not my thing, but I was not a stranger to the funk either.

During one of her visits to the class, she stopped by my table, looked at my progress on my birdhouse and mustered up the courage to ask, "So how do you feel being the only black guy in this class? Ain't it weird?"

I played it cool and downplayed how weird I often thought it was. I said, "Nah, I like standing out." As I kept on with my work, I could see I had her attention by not giving her a lot of attention which stirred the stubbornness in her personality and made her want to fight for it.

She then added a sprinkle of assertiveness to her next statement. "Well, you're doing more than just standing out, you're more like the elephant in the room."

I snickered at the joke and then looked up at her and playfully said, "Dang I wonder why?"

She then whispered in my ear with "I think it's because you're Black."

I replied sarcastically with "Thanks for letting me know. Everything makes sense now."

She laughed with a slight snort and said, "I like this kid."

She then skipped away like a doe, leaving a scent of perfume behind.

As time went on I would see her in the halls and we would talk in passing. One day we found ourselves in the hall alone. She saw me and asked how my day was. I always liked it when girls were as comfortable with small talk as well as deep conversation. I replied and returned the question. Somehow the conversation went from cracking jokes, and talking about fighting, to dancing.

She asked if I ever line danced before, then she grabbed my hands and placed one behind her at her lower back and held my other hand up high like a trophy and she said, "Let's dance."

We playfully spun around in the hall and forgot whatever reasons we had excused ourselves from class in the first place.

She would occasionally look up into my eyes, smile and tell me something I wasn't doing right. I would just laugh and shake my head.

Then the mood turned gray. She stopped.

Looking down and away saying, "My parents would kill me if I dated a black guy."

Standing still, the hall felt like it was still swaying and turning like we once were.

I had no idea how to respond.

Perfect harmony?

THE MOST DEDICATED

I must confess I wouldn't be feeling this way if I wasn't talking about you.

There's two phrases in the English language that I want you to hear.
I love you
and
I'm proud of you...

I pray that God blesses your mother's womb for having you, then multiply that blessing on your womb for having me.

As the seed, I can attest that the soil from which I sprouted was rich and fertile.
I'll call you Mother Nature because you're the nature that nurtured me. The only mother I know.

You're the vessel of pottery the potter formed to carry me and if He knew me in your womb,
then I could imagine what He thinks of you.

I imagine God calls you up like old friends do when you cross His mind,
just to check on you from time to time,
and He tells you He's coming back soon
and you snug the phone up between your ear and shoulder blade and tell Him alright,
I'll fix You a plate.

NEWTON'S LAW

Newton's Law of Inertia says,

"An object that's in motion will remain in motion, but an object at rest will remain at rest."

I've spent a lot of time as an object at rest.

Every day, on my way back and forth to work,
I drive past a bus stop with a homeless man growing out of it.

I tell myself I'll try to motivate him one day,
but in all honesty,
I'm no different than he is,
and I shouldn't lie to myself in thinking that my 9 to 5 sets
me apart.

In all actuality we are both the same,
we've both let dreams die,
and we've both become complacent.

I remember a time in my life where air tasted better than
any food I could eat,
I would hold it on my tongue before it filled my core like a
balloon.

I found the air tasted like gratitude,
and I couldn't get enough,
so much so that if gravity would let the string anchoring

me to earth go,
I would probably float up and away until I became a blur,
then a speck, then no more.

But now, sometimes the air tastes stale like
disappointment and regrets.

Newton's Law of Inertia says,

"An object that's in motion will remain in motion,
but an object at rest will remain at rest."

I can't spend any more time as an object at rest.

THIS KINDA LOVE

There's a look I'm looking for.
The expression of when you realize that your real eyes
have made contact with real eyes, like contacts
over real eyes.

When our souls finally touch in a Michelangelo kinda way
and we've contracted a disease known as attachment
and decided to throw the cure out of the window
while joyriding
in a car with no brakes.

In revelry, we'll break three laws in one night.
Littering.
Loitering each other's premises.
And kidnapping.

Then we'll hold our hostages for ransom.
And ask for a price that neither of us can pay.

GOOD MEN: A POETIC SHORT

There is a dire need
for fathers,
scholars,
hard workers, and
farmers...

Those who plant seed
and return for harvest.

Truth be told,
the fields are plenty
the crops are many,
but the dedicated are few.

There is a dire need
for good men
to cultivate the youth.

ON THAT DAY

On that day
when life has finally etched its story on my wrinkling canvas
and my bones creak under my weary weight,
I will go faithful unto my Master's arms
as young and full of spirit as the day I came.

And death will tire taking me
and still find no victory,
and death will tire taking me and still find no victory.

WORDS

Words have power.
Words carry weight.
Words brought light into darkness,
life into existence,
and started the time clock of our fate.

Now here we are.
Fast forward to where
we get so bent out of shape
over he say she say
when we are only responsible
for what we convey.

So, therefore,
I express whatever,
I believe whenever,
I. Say.
My words can tell you the sky is purple,
my words can run circles around the goggles of Steve Erkel.

Heal you or hurt you
bless you or curse you
teach you bad habits
or instill in you virtues,
but this should not be you, see.

My words are a reflection of an ongoing war inside of me,
a war of which its collateral is contradiction.
But what if only *Dasani* flows out of this estuary?
What if my words planted and watered seeds
into the soil known as your soul
and gardens grew?

And from those gardens kingdoms rose
and flourished with love and prosperity,
with verbal clarity, my words would paint pictures.

Masterfully I would create tapestries,
allude to the galaxies.

With each gasp
I would take you to faraway places,
introduce you to unfamiliar faces,
point out the traces
of a love so unimaginable
and yet get you to imagine
that it's because of that love
the stars lean in closer
and shine brighter for you, my listener.

The wind blows calmer for you.
The leaves fall gentler for you.
The birds sing louder for you.
My words would build up not tear down.
My words would be the fine grit sandpaper that smooths
over callousness,
the peace treaty that ends wars of recklessness.

If this was all possible would these just be my words?

WHAT CAN I OFFER THEM?

I watched as silhouettes
bent on ill intent
wade through the black velvet thickness of the night.
From the distance
I heard a plight,
a voice pitched in a minor key
hitting notes of consensual defeat,
a single mother.
Single-handedly making attempts
to stand on her own two feet
while raising two kids who now stand
just over two feet.
By selling her wares
for money, food, rent,
and the crack she now needs.

My eyes leak
as I think
back to a time when I was reppin' single digits
trying to sit still,
because my mamma told me not to fidget
ridin' in the backseat,
of her *Cutlass Supreme*.
My eyes gazing through the window
at the broken, hopeless, and fiends.
Thinking, *What do they need?*

Baby, it's "Jesus, Jesus, Jesus!"
my mamma would plead.
I'm now a grown man
and these three words have planted a seed.
And that seed has now matured
into a fruit bearing tree,
whose roots draw living water.

From the Word of God I now read.
So what can I offer them?
Nothing to fill my pockets,
but freedom from sin.

Listen
this ain't my logic,
let Him live within,
let Him make a deposit,
you can cash it in.

Store up heavenly treasure
receive of a grace and mercy
that's given without any measure.
As you abide in Him,
find out your precious and treasured.
Remember His faithfulness and remained faithfully tethered.

BROKENNESS

What of such brokenness?
The way circumstances come crashing down on
creaking bones
like the sound used wood flooring makes
as aged planks support teetering body weight.

The kind of brokenness found in
tear-drenched pillow
muffled conversations
with the one whose burden is light as stoic walls
in your secret places of confession eavesdrop while your
deepest parts make their escape from trembling lips
like warm breath that slips out of shivering bodies in the cold.

We grow so desperate to feel what already lies
within our being.
We face our seasons of winter with an impatient childlike
desire for spring.
It is here we are the most honest with ourselves and
the most honest with God.

BEFORE

I once had a fighting spirit.
Before fractured encounters with jagged edged souls took
pieces of me with them because hurting people hurt people.

Before choir processions
sang about how our blessings are coming, they're on their
way,
and all I can do is wish they were here because if I hold my
breath any
longer I will become a balloon and float away.

Before I've seen more funerals than weddings,
before it took more than my fingers and
toes to count up all of my losses.

Before my heart began to feel like a dumbbell that lands on
my chest with the weight of the world at both ends and
I'm not able to crank out that one last rep.

Before my tears became so heavy that
when I cry I lose water weight.
And each drop that hits the floor sounds more like hail than
rain...

Feels more like hell and pain.
Hurts more like pangs and strain.

BREAK

The tension still remains,
but the dust is beginning to settle.

We are at our worst,
and you clutch a mirror
as you powder your nose
while I drink my half-empty glass of pain.

Only one of us truly wants to make up, but neither
of us will break.

GUIDANCE

Young men become old
void of old men to lead them.
Old men remain young.

ST. LOUIS

Gunshots fill night air.
Mothers hold limp lifeless frames.
Broken hearts need hope.

THIS BEAUTIFUL DAY

I see birds dancing between tree limbs prancing,
as the wind held their branches up high,
and their trunks just below the waistline
to remind us why summer leaves slowly sway.

The sunlight squeezed between slits in the window blinds and
stole kisses from my face
on This Beautiful Day.

I'VE BEATEN THE ODDS

I'd like to believe that every day I wake up and
take my first breath,
my feet touch the cold floor sending signals through my
core that remind me I have beaten the odds.

I'm young and I'm black and
statistically speaking I have a 75% chance of extinction.

But by the grace of God I can proudly say I am beating the
odds.

Should there be a mountain of prejudice,
a canyon of hatred,
or perks of privilege outside of my grasp,
I lay claim to each milestone that testifies I have beaten the
odds.

That even the state of my soul
adheres to the path of eternity because
sin and death are odds I have also been given victory over.

When the world predicts my fate to meet my demise at the opposing end of the barrel,
caught between hues of blue and blood,
choir singing *"His Eye is On the Sparrow,"*
he died far too young,
mother crying rivers over the body of a setting son,
his soul now dancing over clouds in heavenly freedom,
either way I will live or die as one who has won
because I have beaten the odds.

PRE-EXISTING LOVE

I loved you before you realized it.
Before our eyes reflected starry night skies
and caterpillar cocoons hatched into butterflies in our
stomachs.

I know it's a lot to stomach.
But I loved you before you figured out this was love.
Before your heart played that syncopated jazz and your
head continued to do the math, crunch the numbers,
adhere to all logic and reason then advise otherwise.
I loved you.

Before I thought about stealing your heart.
Before you thought about giving it away.
Before roses became red and violets became blue,
and sparks flew
And your skin took on rosy-like hues.

Before I occupied your thoughts
and the corners of your mouth would reach up toward your
eyes.

Because this love gave you another excuse to smile
As if you hadn't had enough excuses already.

SHADES OF BLACK

I set out to write a sonnet.
I found out all my thoughts
were violent.
Colors of black clash against shades
violet.
Images play behind closed eyelids
but spiritual eyes stay open.

I'm hoping for certain
the curtain will close
on my game of charades that's getting old and I'll be forced
to save fakery for yet another day.

Because I can't hide from You
I can't hide the truth.
We haven't spoken in a few.
Cold shoulders turn into about faces
but yet You remained faced with
all of my insecurities
and tendencies to put my intricacies
over Your love for me.

Tomfoolery if I ask You.
Too bad I haven't lately.
And now my heart hates me.
I've been a barren wasteland in need saving,
in need of crosses and crucifixions.

Blood on cloth
like soap on sponges
to blot out my guilty convictions
or wash these dirty dishes.
Maybe these scriptures could
replace images of vixens,
eyes full of lustful intentions.

HERE AM I

I have war in my head
peace in my bed,
the Good Book perched on my nightstand,
and a morgue in my closet.

I was born a mortician by nature.
But I read somewhere that
You once brought dead men back to life,
welcomed thieves into Your home,
made lovers out of murderers,
and wrote Your enemies in as beneficiaries of Your will,
then died so they can inherit Your wealth.

I think often about going to heaven when truth be told,
it's only two bent knees and a nightstand away.

A FINAL NOTE

I want to be remembered
like fading embers remind one
of a former flame
once faith and hope filled my country tis of thee
this land of liberty
now shamed by iniquity and defamed.

In the event of my demise
I want to be remembered
for equality to all men
in plurality and morality.

IN GOD WE TRUST?

Yet the knife we thrust
when we fail to utter His name.

In the event of my demise
I want to be remembered not as a tyrant
not as an insinuator of
confusion, strife, and violence.

Yet the violent take it by force
this strange doctrine has strayed my course.

The ship has sailed.
The ship HAS SAILED!
THE SHIP HAS SAILED!

without...
Any...
Sails...
Sails...
Sail, that so-called star-spangled banner of hope is now
a stretched blanket over fifty orphaned children seeking
thirteen deceased parents.

Lady Liberty is a foster mother working three jobs to make
ends meet.

And it's the ends that justify the means so the likelihood
those ends would ever cross paths is slim to none.

Where's the one?
I need a hero.
My demise is approaching zero.
I'm just delaying the inevitable.
Deaths' timing is impeccable.
My fate was sealed when disobedience was found edible.
I feel it.
Me fixed in their reticle.

POW!

In the event of my demise,
when my heart can beat no more,
I hope to die for a principle,
a belief I have lived for.

Please support the Student Writers Studio.

Student Writers Studio is a nonprofit 501(c)(3) organization in St. Louis. The mission of Student Writers Studio is to empower, enrich, and encourage students through their development as writers. We serve students in Grades 3-12 in several programs: afterschool writing classes, writing tutoring, and publishing. We want to see students across the St. Louis area recognize their writing potential and use writing as a tool to instigate change in themselves and in their communities. Our afterschool writing classes teach students different creative genres of writing, such as spoken word poetry, short stories, playwriting, and more. In our writing center, volunteer tutors work one-on-one with students to administer tailored lesson plans, helping students develop creative and academic projects. Students can have their written works from the classes and writing center published in Student Writers Studio's anthology. Students learn how to be curious and engaged in their writing, how to implement creativity and form a unique writing voice, how to be confident in their abilities, and how to critically think through their writing process.

To support our programs,
give on the Student Writers Studio website at:
http://www.studentwritersstudio.org/take-action/donate/
or through the $SWSFund at
https://cash.me/app/RVVDFWB.

ABOUT THE AUTHOR

Gabriel Desince has a heart for youth and empowers them in finding their purpose through creative writing, reciting poetry and sharing messages of authenticity, hope and wellness through life experiences. As a Boarding School Administrator and Therapeutic Music Facilitator, he's provided safe, artistic space for positive expressions. He's worked with teen sex offenders and felons as a Youth Rehabilitation Director. As the Founder of Network and CHILL (Collectively Handcrafting Intentional Lifelong Leaders) he seeks to unite and teach youth how to operate in the professional world.

Gabriel Desince is the author of Broken Pieces, a collection of introspective poems crafted to be the vulnerability others don't want to be.

For spoken word, presentations or to connect with the author:

FB: Gabriel Desince
IG: Memorablemantras
LinkedIn: Gabriel Desince

Printed in the USA
CPSIA information can be obtained
at www.ICGtesting.com
LVHW041415041024
792843LV00006B/1173